NOTES TO THE BELOVED

MICHELLE BITTING

NOTES TO THE BELOVED

All Rights Reserved

Printed in the United States of America

First Edition

2 3 4 5 6 7 8 9

Selections of up to four lines may be reproduced without permission. To reproduce more than four lines of any one portion of this book, write to C&R Press publishers John Gosslee and Andrew Sullivan.

For special discounted bulk purchases please contact C&R Press: sales@crpress.org

Notes to the Beloved
Copyright © 2017 by Michelle Bitting

Cover and design by James Meetze
Cover art: "Ostracism" by Eugenia Loli
Typeset in Crimson with Summer Heart titles

ISBN-13: 978-0-9831362-3-1
LCCN: xxxxxxxxxx

C&R Press
Conscious & Responsible
www.crpress.org

for Phil
and for Dorianne

CONTENTS

ONE

MY BUKOWSKI LIFE 15
MAMMARY 16
PERMEABLE, SMITTEN 18
MOTHER'S DAY OMEN 19
IN PRAISE OF MY BROTHER, THE PAINTER 21
THE RAISED SHADE OF MORNING 22
ON THE LOWER WEST SIDE 22
ON ANY DAY LIKE ALICE 24
MORNING, HIGHWAY 126 25
WASHED IN FLAME 26
ON THE MERITS OF LINGERIE 27
ROBERTSON BOULEVARD ONRAMP 28
HIS HAT 29
BAPTISMAL 31
THE DESIROUS ACT OF LOOKING 33
PATTI SMITH 35
OBSESSION 38
AND IN THAT MOMENT I WAS HAPPY 39
METEOR 40
BLACK GUITAR 42
MAD AT ME? 44
SKINNY DIPPING 47
AROUND THOSE HOUSES UP THE HILL 48
IN ROOM 242 50
PERSIMMON 54

TWO

THE CALL 59

SHERIFF 61

DON'T LOOK NOW 62

BIRTH 64

EPIPHANY 65

STASH 67

BOYS LIKE YOU 69

AFTER FOUR DAYS
OF HAMMERING RAIN 70

BROTHER BLUES 71

HAPPY 72

ANNIVERSARY 74

NEWMAN'S OWN 75

BERYL MERCER, ACTRESS 77

OPEN IN CASE OF 79

NO DIRECTION HOME 81

TRANSITIONS 84

SUPERMAN 86

AND LOVE SHALL REIGN ABOVE ALL 89

THE PRODIGAL WIFE RETURNS 92

WHEEL OF FORTUNE 93

IF YOU CAN'T BE WITH THE ONE YOU LOVE,
HONEY 96

IN THE GARDENS OF ESALEN 98

FAULKNER FARMS 100

NO MATTER 102

ACKNOWLEDGMENTS 107

NOTES TO THE BELOVED

ONE

*...and sometimes in private,
my kitchen, your kitchen,
my face, your face.*
—Anne Sexton

My Bukowski Life

Again, the dream where I run away.
Having shed my Good Doll life,
I tuck myself downtown: slum
dog vestibule, the song of my neighbor
retching next door. Through tobacco-stained
glass, brick chimneys stacked like cakes
sugar the skyline. Now the silk pillow
of a cloud floating past. No one knows me here.
I'm bland as an apricot: six of one,
half a dozen another. I should be afraid
but cockroach caulking doesn't scare,
nor the fact my children hate me,
my stomach growls, nor the endless
seep of brown water from upstairs,
the stain on the ceiling
I see each morning my eyes
pop wide as magnolias. I no longer speak,
though my mouth is stuffed
with words. It's the equation of
a dragon spewing fire in reverse:
I inhale smoking vowels, digest
flaming verbs. My arm becomes a tail,
my pen, the striking tip. When ink
touches paper, this page, she burns.

MAMMARY

Hawks circle fields near the highway
homing in to catch the scent
of animals deep in the high dry grass.
So many wildflowers in bloom,
watery purples and acid yellows,
I'm dizzy in my car
blazing up the California coast:
Santa Barbara, Pismo, Salinas,
nicknamed *The salad bowl of the world*
with its patchwork plots
of endive and spinach,
the almighty artichoke
in whose honor
Norma Jean Baker
was once crowned queen.
So fresh in her red gingham blouse,
remember? Her elation,
her perky, generous D cups
held up to the leafy bulbs
as everyone cheered. If only
it stayed so rosy, the tough layers
unstripped, the heart left intact.
If only you weren't topless
on a gurney, Rachel,
under the scouring glare
of hospital lights,
your own sweet breasts
offered up to the surgeon's blade.

A hundred miles north
of where you are right now
I'm a slave to this shifting view,
anything to avoid the thought
of your chest picked clean,
tender globes that fed three mouths,
now poison the body's crop.
I imagine birds and flight
as the elliptical sweep of sharpness
cuts the pale sky of your chest,
steel beaks of surgical tools
carving out the flesh cream,
making smoke of tumor meat—say goodbye,
pay my respects
and picture them floating up,
slipping through the ceiling cracks:
two blond angels,
flying out
beyond the moon's milky scar,
they spread their innocence
over the lustrous scrim of L.A.,
those brave, radiant girls
wave and then they're gone.

PERMEABLE, SMITTEN

Piped in Lennon penetrates veins, ignites
obsession. I become sound, a black box speaker
tipped to kiss stage floor, deaf dancer
pirouetting on the boom beat of desire,
her percussive metatarsals. Oh to buzz about
something else, rearrange the marquee. Your role
not stroking the fine hairs of my spine, just so.
The after show remains unseen: a room
at the Chateau Marmont, my naked knees
reciting Keats every which way. Reservations
we'd press from wet ashes of our burning houses.
Strange, how I've never loved my husband,
bare-fleshed in the kitchen, more. Your eyes,
a feast of saints, my hands inhaling two worlds.

MOTHER'S DAY OMEN

Come, love, undress me anyway,
let your fingers fly
to my ruddy buttons,
my lips to your opened
underworld. The children,
cocooned in beds,
are dreaming of turtles
in iron canyons. The cat can watch
for all I care, here,
in the living room, where propped
pillows and candle glint
conjure palaces. Imagine
ruling my empire of thighs, laying
siege to my sunken tomb.
On my knees, with you
behind, the gold brocade
of your dead aunt's rug
embeds its fleur across my brow.
We both know I don't deserve it—
dust conspires on the mantle,
a lost peach grows green fur
in the fridge's hoary crypt.
But, listen, love,
love me anyway.
You see those shimmering dots
glowing through the snot-smudged windows?
They could be eyes
of the dog I saw yesterday:
coyote mama driven down

from the bull-dozed hills.
She was lost, zig-zagging
the streets, her swollen teats
jiggling nervously towards traffic.
And the mailman and I
stood there, dumbstruck,
passing envelopes between us.
Not caring, not wanting to know
whatever bad news it was
she was trying to deliver.

IN PRAISE OF MY BROTHER, THE PAINTER

How every morning he rose, slave
to the sound, this endless call to make.
Mad hatter, dervish sawyer, a primitive
blur of hands at work: fingers feeding
the dreamiest bolts through needles,
vision's machinery. In the photo where
he stands, fists on hips—defiant, electric
in his Bowery studio, splotched jeans
and boots, the clouds of white gesso
a kind of palette couture—so satisfied
his look: *Je suis arrive, Asshole…*And
this is how I want to remember him.
Not what a note left like that means.
Not the slow descent, the pills or piles
of soiled laundry. Not the dog left barking
in the kitchen, the bowl with enough grain
to last. No, I want the beauty, even
his cursive, the swirling tints
of parting thought, the art itself: *Dear Sister,
if I could survive this long, you will flourish.*

THE RAISED SHADE OF MORNING ON THE LOWER WEST SIDE

From what must be the most beautiful view
in New York City, you can watch boats unzip
the long blue bodice of the Hudson,
white boas of churned up feathers dragged
in their frothy wake. Cars rush uptown or downtown,
east to west, but only one way or the other
and you must choose on any given street
unless you are a bird: a sparrow, finch,
seagull, or ordinary pigeon, in which case
you can flap and dive and flutter
at whatever height, speed, or aerodynamic
configuration, sail with the wind or against it
if you want to get where you are going.
You are a bird and so above the laws
of ordinary traffic, of ordinary human.
What's human is to have a heart
like a bird that soars and sweeps
and flickers to the consternation
of those left standing on the dock below,
waving their arms
while the tea in their thermoses
turns cold. The audacity of flight.
The fact of the airborne heart,
that gritty, wet red engine revved
and releasing itself from the sky's bright palm,
weaving around the dim side of ships
and skyscrapers, flower stands and taxi cabs,

the dread-locked silhouette of a man
on the corner filling the acapella air
with a sound lovelier than you could
ever imagine waking up to this morning,
the heart, its bent ears shivering,
the trees in the high park rustling,
their leafy nests and shadowed landings
where the heart, for all its regal
and wildly ecstatic pumping, eventually sleeps.

ON ANY DAY LIKE ALICE

No reason to think it wouldn't happen,
then it did. Fault of a loose bootlace
and slipping, her hands groping
for solid ground. Free-fall. Swirling
vertigo of tree roots, beetles,
of green tarantula nests stranded,
catching hold of her hair's
arpeggios. Paisley blouse opening,
the fission of buttoned eyes. To fall
and fall and fall, tug of thick silt,
iron pudding heaving as she hurled
towards the heart. Escape velocity,
imploded planet—mother open,
swallowing the blue pill of her body.
Day, a smoldering crack barely visible
overhead, an angel dissolved. She crossed
herself mid-flight and fell, far
from the known address,
everything until then
that held her to its surface.

MORNING, HIGHWAY 126

Farmers heft and truckers load crates
of lemons onto flatbeds at first light.
The skillet trees stream past,
silhouettes of yellow fruit and shadowed green
like something aquatic. Here I go,
sucked under, again. I love what won't
belong to me
and so sit tight, fingering
the wound, the open sinew,
sticky gem pot
in the lap of the matter.
At any moment, my heart a bowl
of pabulum, stirred or eaten.
Flimsy houses whiz by
the flanks of my eyes, jimmied
plank to dust
by the cranks of decline.
I drive while reason takes a hike.
Let me spin, I say.
Let me crumble in your hands,
my raw materials, my soil
ganged up on. You
and your gorgeous worms
that won't stop working on it.

WASHED IN FLAME

*And no one can still recognize the woman washed in flame
for whom, of all her joys, burnt pearls in ashes is the sum
of what remains.*
—Abraham Sutzkever

>You make a matchstick of your finger,
>dunk the tip in Bombshell Red.
>Then your lips are two flickers,
>in the shadows of your ears, smoldering
>flowers. You draw a smoky line
>between lid and lash and dash out—
>at the crowded rear of the oncologist's elevator,
>one last fanning of your mahogany skirt.
>Don't try to follow the logic,
>this need for ritual preening, seduction,
>whether the doctor's even aware
>of silk swishing between your legs.
>It's pointless, futile as asking why
>your cells' crooked kindling
>camp their deadwood
>deep in your body's core.
>Just remember the pretty Polish girl
>pinching her cheeks for the German soldier.
>*Zierpuppe*, he said, lifting her onto the truck.
>As if it mattered her eyes were two hazelnuts,
>her skin, beaded milk. *So lovely, so worth saving,
>am I not?* And he, head cocked, smiling,
>pretending not to know
>what awaited her, further on up the road.

ON THE MERITS OF LINGERIE

My friend has her breasts removed;
I rediscover lace. Lady-in-waiting
bedside, I keep vigil as sutures settle,
thrust two forearms under blanketed
knees so she can scoot upright,
sip meatball soup fetched, still steaming.
Back home, dig an ancient teddy
from the crypt of forgotten garments
and glide into pitch satin,
remembering how I'd lost my way
weaving back from the cafeteria,
self-recriminations concerning vanity,
the body's tyranny. Brand new hospital
and many rooms empty. Fresh carpet,
paint—pristine wings ignorant
of suffering to come: incessant thumbs
pressed to morphine buttons. My friend was dozing
when I found her again, a few wisps
of gray dream fallen to one side
of her smooth crown. That night
my husband brandished his flesh
and I fell on it, more in love suddenly
than I'd recalled, reaching
down for the little curtain:
I swept aside black silk and let death enter.

ROBERTSON BOULEVARD ONRAMP

First a spark, then flames of floral consensus.
We're a patch on a hill under a freeway

with enough mineral seepage to start a yellow riot.
A thousand button heads bowed beneath

the concrete proscenium—roar of idling engines
and the screech-hiss-honk we've come to hear

as applause. Just look at those cars lining up.
Eyes cast on us not the road. We're candy

for the weary and ground-trodden, lemony pearls
at the city's soot-stained feet. In the quotidian

straits of rush hour, where boulderday meets
bouldernight, we dash the blues with our siren

show, landscape boosting nerves
for the long drive home. No need to thank us;

we thrive on simple gifts. Bouquet to the world
of sun-stung blossoms, our own standing ovation.

HIS HAT

Anyone can wear a porkpie,
don a jaunty straw boater
or felt fedora,
crook the hound's tooth lip
of a mini Stetson
over a martini-flogged eye
and blot the day's sun,
its blistering news.
But if you are Johnny Depp,
your hat is more
than a statement of style,
more than a rakish blend
of old and pop-world panache,
more than a plaid bucket,
a hobo pan inverted,
a drapery cage to quiet
the inner flutter
of your imaginary world. It is
the devil's haberdashery,
the kind reserved for
a breed of noble idiot,
of holy jester,
with enough ink in his royal aura
to grease the stations of the cross.
You are the perfect
modern imposter: barber, sailor,
mob man, chocolate maker,

and your timeless face
of stopped-clock beauty,
the milk bone stalk
of your neck, the broken worm
moustache and fuzzy goatee,
horn-rimmed glasses
that frame your Buster Keaton
peeps, your silly swagger
and beggar's humility,
sweeten the sting of everyday living.
Johnny, if you can hear this,
know I've got your button
pinned to my heart
and I'll do what it takes—
brave the high salty seas,
ride the wing of your private jet
as it caroms between Paris
and the Bahamas—I'm here
to hold you up, whatever finery
you may be sporting, honey,
I've got an excellent rack.

BAPTISMAL

Now that summer's gone,
flung into earth's bony bed.

Now that she's packed her flask
of Night Thunder

and like a callous lover skipped town,
offered up her plump

and seedy Heirlooms,
the endless tumblings of tousled

grass, the lemon necklaces
left to rot—

I can talk about love,
the way you broke and entered me,

made everything new. While it's true
that whale on the horizon

could be a sign
I may be swallowed

as fire sweeps the rifled fields,
heaven rains ice,

the Devil whisking
his scarlet cape, carrying off

my pungent crops,
or a black curtain of locusts

descends to shroud me blind.
And priests will drone on

about babies most fiercely wired
with Satan's zeal,

swaddled over the rippled
font, scream loudest

as water cascades down
their bulbous, talced brows.

Well, then there's me
on the Highway to Hell,

throat open and heart full throttle,
plumes of metallic smoke

marking the air and dust
with strange signs, because

really, in your naked,
sacred company, Darling,

who would want to be saved?

THE DESIROUS ACT OF LOOKING

(after Titian's Venus of Urbino)

You think you know me: *meretrici, cortigiana,*
whore—a girl willing to shed her corsets,

serve the artist's opulent eye. And it's true:
getting by on a scullery's wage, the few

coins tossed for a back-alley tryst
won't stop my stomach shriveling

to grape-size, won't keep my curves
this plush. I'm heavy cream in these sheets,

tresses tickling breasts with their rills
of coiled gold. Naked here, nunneries are distant—

a cruel, irrelevant joke. Crude as a noble lady's
life, stuffed away in her marital tower,

bereft of news or geographical sense, stiff
black gown and rosary inspiration for nooses.

Perhaps you think I lack propriety: too
sexy to be chaste, and those women behind me,

craned over *il cassone*, frantic for my tossed
dress, are instructed to guard my shame.

So you've ignored the ring *d'oro*,
lights up my teeniest finger, my faithful

spaniel *Fido*, snoring away at my tapered feet.
Perhaps won't believe when I touch myself

down there with one hand, pink roses
bloom in the other. Or that my husband

summoned this portrait, the word *goddess*
a radiant jewel dotting the crown

of my *yes, yes, yes*! Anymore than you
might admit, Dear Viewer, as I gaze

from the canvas, and your eyes refuse
to leave—the desirous act of looking is mutual.

PATTI SMITH

(after the premiere of "Dream of Life")

On the street outside The Aero Theatre,
two women puzzle
under the late summer stars,
dumbstruck in their Loreal lips
and pastel sweaters
by the unconventional allure
of the Godmother of Punk.
Where is the beauty,
they are wondering, about
her mannish mug,
the razor chin
and dingy teeth,
her unshaved pits,
the way she stomps around the stage
in heavy black boots,
her faded peace sign t-shirt
drenched with rock star sweat.
What is it about her,
blindfolded, arms raised,
clapping to the hellfire
heavens as the audience belts
the soaring refrain:
G—l—o—r—i—a...Gloooooria!
like some ecstatic shaman,
whiskers of white spittle
sprouting down her chin.
She's spewing Rimbaud,
Ginsberg, Baudelaire,

a long silver cross
slung across her chest,
as the airborne audience
howls and stamps its collective feet,
the wings of her scraggly hair
flapping open and shut
around her urgent, transfixed face.
Singer or saint? Like me,
these ladies want to know,
as they fumble for their keys,
yakking away as cars buzz past
and the red marquee fizzles out.
They want to know
but there are no answers,
only the rush
of being baptized
for two cinematic hours
in the golden showers
of a factory girl from Jersey
who moved to New York City,
opened her cowboy mouth cave
and felt it ripen,
burst like a grape
in the cosmopolitan sun.
Don't you wish you wrote
those wild, edgy songs,
trashed the Chelsea Hotel
with Sam Shepard,

CBGB's and going platinum
only to take the money
and run to raise two kids
in the suburbs of Detroit?
In your fifties you re-emerge,
reinvent yourself,
rock 'n rolling the world stage
from Seattle to Berlin.
And when you're not
chanting for crowds,
inhaling a microphone
or fondling the pebbly contents
of an ancient Persian urn
filled with Mapplethorpe's ashes,
you are tracking Blake's ghost
through the cemeteries, parks,
and urinals of Paris,
every place his bony,
misunderstood ass
is known to have squatted
and scribbled something beautiful
while taking an ordinary,
everyday, entirely human piss.

OBSESSION

There's a rickety trellis
winds down
its flowered center,
blistered with cobalt,
the satin innards
of a magician's sleeve.
To climb it is to waste not one iota of life.
To climb it is to find the sister lost to the drowning pool.
To climb it is to waterfall under
a white apron of stars,
shoot the foamy, forbidden dam
you risked to thrill
that summer at camp.
How your mouth became an exploding tent,
the river tucking each scream
inside its watery pocket.
And how much older you felt
traveling back,
the tent finally collapsing,
the bus that chugged on
with no sound left,
your eyelids sandbagged,
your head's smoky knuckle
leaned into glass,
rapping the night
as sleep took you down
and whatever dream you couldn't shake
held you under
its long road home.

AND IN THAT MOMENT I WAS HAPPY

What year it was I can't remember
when the clocks froze I lost track
then woke to find myself prone
full-bodied, tan, on an ideal beach,
sea-shells like smooth white berries ticking away
the collapsed island hours. Even the faces
of beloveds sewn up for now
inside heavy orbs, fruit that sways, oiled
and persistent from tropical branches
until villagers shake them down
and dam the creeks so the children can swim.
I am going nowhere and I like it.
I, a spindle around which salted blue
marimbas, reconstructing heaven,
branding me with vision, the right to overthrow
the cave, the casket past, the possibility of crows.

METEOR

Oh to have been in Canada
when the pieces fell
to earth, the fireball late Thursday
over Saskatoon—billion-watt bulbs
                     bursting
*shook the house
and sounded like dinosaurs walking,*
                          well…only once
in a thousand births
do mamas land their molten babes like that,
most burn up, entering. Dumb luck
      orbits
             around
and we line up—divine, bedeviled.
                     In California,
a woman in a gown
the color of crude oil
is stranded on a road outside Palm Springs
and thinks *emergency*,
pointing her flare gun at the stars.

      Red flags rocket, smoke, fizzle,
        then disappear into the atmosphere's wallet.

The gorilla suits
will wait by the pool,
full of bling,
stiff cocktails and nuts.

       This is the desert
  where a gimp engine groans
         and coyotes guffaw,
circling the shoulder. Nailed to dust,
        the Christ cactus, dumb,
              stands paralyzed as ever.

Oh lady of perpetual gimme,
desire your way out of this one.

BLACK GUITAR

To pick that glint-edged glamour,
lacquered body, lustrous odalisque,
strung flower. Imagine skipping
my fingers like Dorothy
down its long fretted neck,
enchanted path, inevitable Oz,
the O of sound spinning wild
from that midnight pit. Big obsidian
lung sighing, Billie Holiday's
sheened hip if a hip could sing
and hers could. Every pore
pitch perfect. Notes embossed
on the underside of skin. Even
nostrils, an interior syrup,
run through with primordial
song. I crave this instrument
with cut-away puzzle, missing
curlicue and plug-in potentials.
The way I crave salvation,
a head-long plunge
into amplified abyss, a certain
grunge such beauty requires.
Three squares humiliation
and a stomach for the fall.
Patience, patience. My singing
improves with every hard knock
plucked. Into these arms, Takamine,

my dream true come—strapped on,
tuned up, Lover Man, locomotive,
on your dark-strummed rails
we're forever born to run.

MAD AT ME?

For saying I love you,
for saying your gaze is a bearskin coat
and I'm Zelda Fitzgerald
shaking off the winter chill
at a Princeton football game,
bundling myself up
in double layers of brown fur
and old scotch,
a silver flask and F. Scott's bon mots
folded close to my fragile breast.
Forgive me if the thought of you
makes me wobble in my bleachers,
the mobbed stadium of my heart
rising up to cheer and clap
irrespective of the score
or pigskin meteor,
the open bouquet of a tight end's hands.
I'm prone to exaggerate
and often lack all sense of proportion,
beginning with the very tall blond
in a zebra-striped dress
who just entered this scene,
giving me cause to ponder platinum,
endangered species and wigs.
My menagerie expands
to suit the wilderness demands.
Even last night I pulled the blinds
and tried on costumes. It was good
to slither nude

into the wrap-around kimono
Liz brought from Japan
while a hush darkened the house,
my ears making friends
with flustered crickets under the stove.
I made myself a ready target,
my body spread like moonlight
on the bed's splayed tundra
and fingering the dragon stitching
of my black satin robe,
waited to feed what haunted me.
I've never been to Tokyo,
but almost feel like I have
after watching *Lost in Translation*
how many times, I forget.
Sometimes my heart feels like
an experiment in alien abduction,
probed in broken places
that won't stop bleeding. Sometimes
love is brief but indelible,
a red wax stamp that seals the envelope forever,
mailed off without postage,
the contents still shift,
proving hazardous. My heart
a Komodo Dragon
staring out from a glass box
and I've no idea what to feed it.
The eyes bulge green,
color of sour apples

or the succulent lawns of Los Angeles
where love flares
and falls with the stars
everyday and no one knows
how to drive in the rain. It's all
foot to the metal,
the pavement, the grave,
swerving across glowing yellow,
those broken double lines,
hoping for a head on.

SKINNY DIPPING

There's only so much tension
this blue can hold
before devilish and monkey-batty,
I need to spank its lucid surface,
shed my clammy skins
like a Chiquita banana,
my sickle body,
its nude fruit flung
into undressed air.
What do I know? Only
no Neptune, no Scylla
can control this animal wet,
how it's necessary sometimes
to shovel off dusty
restraint, bolt like a baby
for the frown-free zone.
I'm here to say
a shadowy skeleton lurks
behind this lustrous clock,
its dank fingerprints
already dancing
a dim zodiac down my spine.
Lagoon hussy, river whore,
the cool stroke
of perpetuity is keeping
score inside my wrist
and since there's nothing
water can't heal
or make brand new,
I'll keep throwing myself at it.

Around Those Houses Up the Hill

The bare street glows
under a Haviland bowl moon
and nothing moves until
the wind whips a stray Nordstrom's bag
across Mr. Johnson's lawn
spooking the stray
who doesn't know its place or any better.
A black Lexus of wired teens
laces the double yellow line
and screeches off in a trail
of smoke and Notorious B.I.G.
I remember building forts
in the hills not far from here
with my best friend Velma.
Her father spoke broken English,
tended ground at the private school.
We'd stash boxes of red Jell-o
in our parkas for when
the hard brush-clearing was done.
How our tired muscles trembled
with the rush of cherry sugar
sucked from grubby, wet hands.
Oh people of privilege
and pampered largesse, I hear you
grumbling in your sleep.
Fear not the rank outside,
for your babies sleep cradled in money.
And the apples in your pantry
still exude the winning edge,
their dark dreams illuminated

by the light of captivity,
the lost memory of orchards,
the sweet, democratic scent
of being free and open fruit.

In Room 242

The plumbing backed up
at the Munras Hotel: yellow,
brown-flecked water
filling the sink,
our kids in their jammies,
needing to floss, needing bed.

Lucky the suite next door
lacked occupants,
and our jeans, flip-flops, face cream
stuffed into indiscriminant bags,
we shoved them down the hall—
an impromptu round
of musical rooms
our son could not abide.

This, in spite of his dumpling mug,
quirky humor, still too,
the vast spectrum
of moods, volatile spells,
when faced with sudden change.

They buzz in from nowhere
like the winged-demon
bit my mustang's rump
riding through a grassy, crosscreeked
meadow that time

in Bridgeport, California—
how she bucked and tore off,
dragging me a quarter mile—
my one booted foot
still hooked in the stirrup.

An unpredictable animal, autism.
It rears its wild, baffling head
over trifles: the wrong pop song
streaming an elevator, a kitchen clock
with no advance warning
reset for Daylight Savings,
a familiar bus route switched,
or, like that night,
the numbers on a hotel door
altered by two lousy digits.

There were tears, red tempers
and fists, a gush of screeched
sounds from our sweet boy's mouth.
Words like "twirb" and "focker"
and "shidiot." This newfangled language,
a kind of cockeyed fireworks
from his left parietal lobe.

For an hour we cooed, reasoned,
fought, then dragged him,

four suitcases and a laptop,
his bewildered, barefoot sister,
into our new one-night rent.

When the storm finally settled,
when we'd kissed them to sleep,
saw their eyelids flutter and still
as if flicking the day's
last, troublesome dew,
we stepped out for a smoke—
the balcony quiet
but for the rush
of our slowly exhaled breath
and bickering tongues.

Who was it remembered first
about room 242, still empty,
the key still tucked
in your shirt pocket?

Was it you? Me?
The stars above us
like bravery medals
on God's dark chest,
punishing us
with silver light?
What matters is you took
my hand, slipped your card

into the slot and tumbled us
into sheets, and I rode you,
long and hard to midnight,
one leg pressed
between your shoulder, my sweaty sternum,
the other, a lasso looped
about your lovely, bucking head.

PERSIMMON

Shiny, heart-shaped, orange-red orb.
Pride of Powhatan, the Algonquin
linked tribes, your name sifted down,
re-shaped in the great etymological
cookbook: *putchanin, pessanine,
persimmon*. Last night
I ate you sliced thin, mixed
with pomegranate seeds, a splash
of olive oil, sherry vinegar, salt.
Now I'm a fool for Fuyu.
It was Thanksgiving
at my mother in-law's.
I cooked all afternoon, knowing
disasters loomed ahead: burnt pie,
rogue shards of glass in the gratin,
a scabby remark
about Uncle Bob's heel. And look,
nothing but wine
and snips of Whitman! The children
shoeless, swapping songs,
surfing the Net. Persimmon,
I'm not afraid of you anymore.
Let's beat a drum and dance
buck naked, hunt some deer,
scale a stone cliff,
look wide and far
over a North American plain.

Let's fill our cups
and come together over candles and puddings,
let's praise this life, mere life,
the feast my mouth cries over.

TWO

And what did you want?
To call myself beloved, to feel myself
beloved on the earth.
—Raymond Carver

THE CALL

Most days I wake early
wrapped in miles
of you, mink unfurling
from memory's fist,
from imagined cities
where the waif huddles
in dim-lit tunnels
untangling her baggies
of trafficked gold. My need for this
is great and pendulous.
When was the last time
you touched fur that supple,
stroked the underbelly of want?
Beauty digs its rare nails in:
talons, razor-fine, sprung
from weathered canyons, reflect
grave pleasures I caress,
cast across country, epoch, leaf.
The falcon and the falconer,
who's to say who's king
atop the sharpened branch?
Two fingers gloved as one,
pressed skyward, summon stars
no matter what. Thoughts
swung, thrust at high speed,
a rapid change in direction,
tear the air—delicate strips—and land
in your warm world,

my tongue's ornament. To die
that achingly fresh, called
back to life, a leash, your song,
the unchained route, soaring.
You make it look so easy,
making gods as you go.

SHERIFF

Because the night could sweat you like a bullet,
peel you out of its wrecked, heated flesh
and you'd appear, fresh from some town
where you claim to be mayor only
that word's not sharp enough, Sheriff,
we who strut our consonants hard
and a boy's so much better when he's packing,
black clad, silver chested, the tin star
beaming, its five points flashed
like peaks of trees
at sister planets, yes, from here
I can just see the light
wandering my broken boulevard:
dead center, high noon and loaded,
waiting for you to ride in
and make the bad dream squirm.

DON'T LOOK NOW

When I ran back through the lobby
I was thinking black coffee:
Antigua from a French press
and salted caramels
but you'd already crossed
into shadow, the elevator cave,
your suitcase guillotined
by heavy steel closing in, neck
of a rolling red one,
same as mine. I like that
in the short time I knew you
my mind flew to the Bayou,
then to Venice, even flashed
on that gremlin Donald Sutherland
tracked in the thriller
by Nicholas Roeg, hooded,
crimson-cloaked. What was he chasing?
Something he'd lost
or a sound drowned out
and when he raised his face
to the blue above San Marco,
the Grand Canal dribbled
from a girl in white winched up,
her drenched nightie
a religion some evil
had measured itself against.
I get it. Lost, rushing blind,
like me riding my shopping cart
through foreign lots,
one unlaced Ked crooked
across the metal bridge,

wheels spinning through
lobbies, along water,
chasing something scary,
something sweet
with heat.

BIRTH

Blue yoga ball and mat in tow,
soft spool of boom-box cello
draping hospital drab with Bach,
I sighed and chanted through the tepid cramps
but when the hellish labor hit
I screamed for shots: Demerol, I got,
HMO protocol to stand down pain.
The next hour, a Jimi Hendrix acid trip:
purple haze of morphing faces, gloves,
green masks and rubber hands
zoomed in and out of focus,
my husbands' oozing eyeballs
wet with worry, the blurred white shape
of mother scurrying in the background.
Someone shouted Push!
and my final gears engaged,
the pelvic elevator blooming,
our baby's head galumphing
through the ravaged pit,
my strangling chute, heralded
by a sphincter blast of feces
from my sprung and trumpeting bowels
and we cried "Welcome to the world!"

EPIPHANY

I don't care what my neighbor thinks,
I like to watch my husband
on the lawn untangling
holiday lights. I'm hotter
than a mosquito banging
its legs elastic against
the bare sun of a back porch bulb,
the way my man's out there,
cable muscled between
two clenched thighs,
his lit hands diddling
the red nubs, releasing them
from their knotted misery.
You can hear the grass sigh
as he bends and gathers
his bright world in,
half-moon mouth of a Hanes
Beefy Tee sagged open,
the escaping smoke
of chest hair. Later,
he'll sneak up, pull
me close leaned over
a roast chicken fresh
from the oven's ringed inferno.
Blindsided, I won't know
meat from man: rosemary,
heat, a fine sweat

blasting our tender hips,
spooning the gold juice
so the flavor penetrates,
recurs deep inside
that gnawable dark.

STASH

I read once
that Civil War dolls,
X-rayed for signs
of smuggling drugs
across enemy lines
revealed pits for stuffing opiates:
morphine, enough residue sap
to make a mockery of pain.
I can relate: there were days
that begged nothing more
than a mannequin's smile,
my innards snuggled
by inhibitors, warm blankies
swaddling synapses. Sometimes
the question lingered: whether to smoke,
snort or swallow myself,
decisions dictated by leaky faucets
in ghost towns of my cranium.
When autumn drops,
bearing gusts from Santa Ana,
you can bet there will be fire.
More often now I donate
to the bedroom, your kingdom
of desire, that blue-veined
fullness dangled in my face,
flesh of wild orchids, pain
transposed to a more lyrical
key. Like Johann Sebastian
on the banks of the Rhine,

letting notes fill the rivers
of his hands, then turning back
to compose the world,
map the road aright with song, so
we could keep time
like this, getting high.

BOYS LIKE YOU

Boys like you like to ride on trains
the steady hum of wheels
the rails' endless strum
make splintered neurons
in your brain line up
singing, it's repetition in your eye,
the sweet iteration of color
and shape, trees whizzing by
in cedar clumps, dry grass lots
of parsnips gone to seed, crows
making cursive in the paper sky
flirting or hunting field mice,
at this speed it's hard to tell,
our cokes and hot dogs jostling
and still your gaze stays glued
to the bridges, ducts, ravines,
the concrete overpass
spray painted like fireworks
on backs of houses, porches
hemorrhaging milk crates, old fridges,
propane tanks and laundry lines
rippling faded floral sheets,
a dog on a chain straining
at birds as we dash along
not saying a word, as the world
a mute holy blur rushes past us
and you pray to the window

AFTER FOUR DAYS OF HAMMERING RAIN

In which the troubling thought of sending you away
revisits like a tumor cloud drifting out
of an X-ray's gray and swirling firmament,
we go for a drive—a movie to forget
the tears and fists and shattered glass
and as we round the tree-fringed curve of Sunset Boulevard
where fancy houses float
at the gates of stainless pastures,
pearled and out of reach
of almost everyone
on this battered, hell-plagued earth,
it is still raining, Son,
though bright rays plummet
through the pour,
water and light,
two beautiful wrestlers
duking it out across our windshield,
which makes us smile, the muscles
of contention easing
so that reaching for your hand,
you don't let go or flinch
as something Technicolor arcs
across the sky ahead
and the road before us straightens,
steers us dead on into a turbulent blue.

BROTHER BLUES

— *William Faulkner Bitting 1961-1995*

There's no stopping
this rain, my heart
shaken, dumbstruck leaves
swirled down, memory
flushed to the ground
and my throat damned, again.
Let it loose
sing the trees
but I can't go there, Brother,
my mind won't go there, Brother.
It's enough I carried your
picture around town
all hours today, my satchel
heavy, ghost in the bag.
I carried you like water,
a wounded rain—
you took the pills, you took
yourself away.

HAPPY

Last night there was
that moment in support group,
bare foot slipped between
my husband's crossed thighs,
I felt the roughness of his jeans
scuff my skin. I had nothing
to report but love: nothing but beam,
flambee, tango. Pomegranate martini
and snails for dinner, blissed
in our bistro booth earlier,
inside the globe's grand demise. Look
at the way my baguette sopped up
the yellow oil, weedy slick disbursed into yum.
To think the ocean I grew up with
washed me clean each time
I dove into its dirty lovers' arms
and Daddy, ex-lifeguard, staunch
Republican, taught me how to swim,
his armor of cigar and bourbon pinstripes,
mushy insides sloshing when he'd had
too much to drink. Another brand
of wetness, shock of wine spilled
on parquet, breaking himself open
along with the good china.
Sometimes we'd go
to the fancy French place in Santa Monica:
pink ribbons, red booth and the tide
inside my skin contracting,

my beaches of self-respect suddenly dry,
all crustacean carcasses
and stinky seaweed, odors
bloating in the day's risen heat,
dark nets of swirling sand flies
when he'd bluster, sad bourgeois,
his mispronounced idioms—the maitre d'
biting his tongue, nodding as Daddy
tossed twenties his direction.
This is where I learned
the pleasures of escargots: musky
knuckles, garlic nubs freed
from their spiral houses, hard
as nails or crushed in an instant,
delicious dream I savored
before, inevitably,
saying something stupid,
one of us would ruin it again.

ANIVERSARY

Let our love be asymmetrical. Let it tilt
on its axis, curved in shadow, carved in light.
Let the apple bob and right itself, expose
bruised then brighter sides. Let us not
be wedded to belief in inertia—know
the marriage spins and shifts. Hear how
the heart grinding silent gears, steers
love's fat planet towards unnamed planes
while we slumber on. If we wake
one season behind, and a syzygy of moon,
lake, mantle, makes us crazy,
makes the forest a maze, let us know
there are still fish in the river, my veins'
dark oil, your mouth's red flame—a sky
of lopsided stars to light our way home.

NEWMAN'S OWN

Your ubiquitous head: free-floating,
happy-go-lucky label—
devil blue eyes,
the winning grin that haunts
the aisles, hawking
my favorite salad dressing—
vinaigrette of benevolence
with which I christen the limpest
cruciferous, the most unworthy scallion,
the wimpiest tomato
and still they taste good. Maybe it's knowing
how much you coughed up for clean air,
the huge bite of profit flipped
to help sick children, Sudanese women
who won't be raped
foraging the plains for water. Or maybe
it's only you in *Cool Hand Luke*
and *The Hustler*,
when your chiseled mug first cracked
the big pink peppercorn of my heart.
Maybe it's that you lived with one woman
for fifty years in the spotlight
where love sours,
integrity wilts,
where the cookie never crumbles,
petrified in a Wal-Mart stockroom.

It's nice to have something *genuine*
last—a demi-hero's face
on the supermarket shelf
smiling back in polytheistic splendor,
garlic and basil concoctions
blessed by chapped, heavenly hands.
Except for your funky popcorn,
which my kids say
smells like somebody threw up
in a florist shop, we'll keep filling our carts
with you, Paul, each serving
swallowed, fortified with hope,
our world a little safer
in designated plots,
giving you our sweet applause.

BERYL MERCER, ACTRESS
(b.1882—d.1939)

Time was you could stroll down Hollywood Boulevard
and catch Great Grandma's name
flaming every cherry marquee. In
All Quiet on the Western Front,
Cagney's long-suffering mom
in *The Public Enemy,*
she made the melancholy matriarch
with her ocean liner hips
and squat size, made the big brown
spigots of her eyes open
over a son gone to war
or the devil. What fans didn't know:
how close she lived each sorrow-filled part.
Behind *Musso and Frank Grill,*
trouble rising up
the walls of her Deco loft:
the child lost to polio
before his twelfth birthday;
the no-talent husband who drank
and threw her money at willing starlets;
the illness that took her early
with so many roles to spare. Now here,
on Sunset Boulevard, just shy
of the gem-blue Pacific, I roar past a bank,
gas station, Starbucks, the same plot of land
she got conned into trading
for a Texas font of "tea"

that like so much else went dry. I'm thinking
of her drooped jowls and mouth;
dark hollows below the eyes,
her glum, faraway look
belying a life of presumed glamour,
features my own face mimics
gloomy days when I might be caught
speeding across town, windows wide,
a dry Santa Ana spiriting me
to the *Musso and Frank* bar:
dark-paneled haunt of Faulkner, Chaplin, Fairbanks
and maybe Beryl, who floats in
on her small gossamer wings, finds a stool,
a dry martini next to mine, and leaning
into the microphone of her skewered olive
tells me how it really was,
just how thirsty a girl could get.

OPEN IN CASE OF

The desert beckons as much
as leaving equals a mini gallows,
motel room among coyotes
and Saguaro cactus means
divorce an acre of heart. I miss
my children as much as this
rush to party with flaming sheep
in my soul's black pasture.
What could happen, after all?
My son tanks on his meds,
apocalypse of fits, the house
diminished to a smoky knoll
of burnt pillows, broken snow globes.
Either way, my mind's a zoo,
a cross-wire conundrum
of riposte, eschew. Damned if you do
and if you don't, strung from coils
on a high desert tram. Stay,
stay, rusted to your chair,
practical mama, like the pope,
smiling, icing-white in his cupcake
robe, vapid cherry of bobbing,
sanctimonious head. In your
grid-locked kitchen, the rented
Eden-getaway gone now
that imagined you sprawled
on floral spreads, eared books

and pens scattered, a rat trail
of scribbled paper spilling
from bed onto shag, shade
of avocado. This dream's been
seized again, a wax tableau
in the museum of desire.
Stay, says the voice,
your safe spot by the phone,
warm loom of telemarketers
to cheer you, their shallow,
mechanical pitch, and
that old girl the oven
but a spoon's length away,
sprung mouth open, crying,
See, this way no one gets hurt.

NO DIRECTION HOME

Still recovering from the poison
missive you sent,

curdled fear, a loathing churned up
I'd not felt in years—

Well fuck it, I told the road
who's boss of this night anyway?

And drove on,
the mantra stereo cranked

to Bob Dylan's scouring rants, protested
red, wild-fire, love.

And inside the amplified miles
my eardrums began to burn clear,

blue sneaker to the pedal,
I pressed down hard the cold dread,

speed easing your ill aura
with each highway sign passed—

legions of wings, cake-thick, making
glass graves of my windshield.

When I turned into Granzellas,
that homely, Kitsch-lame hotel,

middle-of-nowhere, Interstate 5,
a bevy of blond chicks

in Southern Bell hats,
slick taffeta, hospitable sheen,

click-clacked across the parking lot:
Someone important in town's getting married

strapped ankles drunkenly squealed
and disappeared

into backseats of Model T's.
So through the gift shop

I drifted, a forest of black jams
and currant syrups spiraling around,

my numb ass finally parachuted
onto a stool at the hotel bar,

the walls of which were inhabited
by every taxidermied creature with horns

ever roamed the range,
bared its teeth. I thought

of your terrible words,
paws the size of pillows, your claw teeth,

thought *Hello my sweet soul in vertigo*
and wondered what would drag me next

to its bell tower lip,
fling me down, free-falling, amazed

to see both my dead self splayed,
a fait accompli, and this me seated here,
mirrored in polished oak,

a checkered napkin spinning my hand
in neurotic circles

as the man working the spigots,
twisted towel at his hip, lolling,

offered to fill me up
with another chipped goblet

of smoky Chardonnay,
his meaty fingers also made

in California
and an animal smile

that knew its own
shade of Noir

but nothing of mine
or yours

and just then,
the only story that mattered.

TRANSITIONS

No other way to describe it:
stepping from the house,
marrying her face
to mist, to air, a state
of in-between, years squeezed,
the juice infused, so many Springs
and what happens next? Cuttings
made of young succulents
nearly fail proof. Dutch bulbs
she dug from the shed
shoved into soil, this random thought,
that plan, buried
in their twenty linked years,
the Hope Whale no longer ridden,
bronco style, along day's
deep undulations but viewed
through painted lenses
from an observation deck,
thin inklings of age
marking space around her eyes
whenever she squinted. Fingers
crossed, flesh forged,
each time he uncrossed her legs
and entered his name,
neither of them knowing
how they'd survive:
world of caved souls,
its dirty greedy light.

Only how pleasure made
the sun strike, the diving bell tremble,
an amen rippling down
another midnight slope,
one tulip shuddering, swallowed up,
a petal pressed between
the mind's purple horizon
and the silence of the field
that made them repeat: let's drink,
cast another hour, another
hand to the bucket. Love's
oblivion is bottomless.

SUPERMAN
(Downtown Los Angeles, ca. 1976)

Perched behind glass
in my father's office,
34th floor of the
Union Bank Building,
I mastered my powers—
penetrated windows,
sailed down the steel facade
to take the city's pulse:
surge of cars, trains, buses,
small as corpuscles
rushing the spindly grids—
the day's random dance
of choreographed chaos.
Father at his desk,
silver bullet of a Tiffany pen
poised above whatever document,
secret as the cryptic patterns
I traced on his tie,
the terse, mysterious words
he fired into the receiver,
gray gravel of his voice
muscling the silence:
Just gimme another minute, Kiddo.
Because it was a school
holiday, because he loved me,
he worked
and I waited, wondered at
the sky's blue cape,
my mind speeding along freeways,

over dirty blond beaches
near our house,
the yellow curtains,
mother there, in her apron
stirring paprika into chicken,
carrots, onion, great clots
of sour cream—
the transplanted recipe
she'd farmed from
her mother's Nebraska kitchen.
Entranced, her spoon
spins circles through
the maze of meat and fat
Is she pondering
a double life as well,
like her man who
stays out too late,
the night's urgent business
calling him
to its lovely side?
My mother knew the face,
knew the snapshot
she'd unearthed one day
from his buckled brief,
the black box opened
and my what a stink
when she did that!
Brother and I fleeing,
slipped into shadows
beneath our beds,

our bodies flat, cast
down to wood and dust,
invisible then
like we'd seen on TV,
little heroes—
we held our breath,
our ears,
and waited
for the foul cloud,
the killing green,
to pass over.

AND LOVE SHALL REIGN ABOVE ALL

It will come back
like a notable comet
burning across turbulent heavens.

Like my friend who didn't scream
when all those bats rushed out of her flue:
I didn't know they were there!

and still she feared not
the dark pattern made on her wall,
instead, embraced the contrast

cast against white molding,
the harmony in difference.
This is my note to The Beloved,

written on scraps that paper
the birdcage in my chest.
Most perplexing: my mother's smile,

its far away galaxy. So too,
the Black Hole of my father's tranquility.
Something shatters this fragile edge,

the gristle bone of forgiveness
and I transcend my cosmic self
from a weed-opulent yard.

When the roots ran rampant
along our shared property lines,
my neighbor suggested we plant fruit trees

in lieu of litigation. I thought
that a helluva great idea
and immediately notified The Pleiades

of our better intentions,
who promptly issued a company memo
to make coming showers

exceptionally stunning. From where I stand,
like those wacky Seven Sisters,
I'm a middle-aged hot B type star

located in the constellation of Taurus
and I can bend this line like Beckham
when I try really hard

and let go, let go,
the way I did that time
in the not-so-distant past

when you licked syrup off
my nipple, ran your tongue around the bumps,
gently teething the hazel stumps

but mostly sucking, the little forest
of sounds that sprang up from my wild,
so loud, so exceptionally green.

THE PRODIGAL WIFE RETURNS

Home at last from the shore and everyone clapped,
the children greeting me, maws wide,
rows of permanent teeth ablaze,
their mouths pried open crypts of alabaster enamel
like resurrected Jesus, his spotlight robes
flung in a blinding flood of white. So happy they were,
every small thing a celebration. Even the teakettle
steamed on the stovetop inside its Calphalon belly
minus twist of knob and Wolf Range flame. My mind

was a valentine, February's pin-up: glossy, buxom,
waxed within an inch of its lush nude life,
there in a garage of broken jalopies. My mind
in a red dress: skin tight with sequins,
every thought a coconut stuffed in its tufted brassiere.
Think of the milk when those babies cracked!
Here, kitty, kitty. Come suck the moist sugars
of higher learning, the sweet sticky trickle
I visit like an office drunk, nipping
scotch from a desk drawer flask.

How else survive the parade today in this café,
the mind-numbing twitter of the stupid mommies
making plans to shop out Fashion Island? Bombs away,
I say! If only to be born caring less, caring only for the hunt,
the wordy cartographer. She'll open the chest,
unleash burgeoning treats. Find the word and the word
is Deliverance. It shall be hers, and hence, all that matters.

WHEEL OF FORTUNE

is what's on tonight
at the nursing home,
cranked so loud, tinitis is certain
if first we don't go deaf.
I could be home right now
ordering take-out: chicken masala,
garlic naan, a spicy lamb curry
and cooling lassi
whose fatty iridescence
is like mangoes
belly dancing in my mouth. If only
my son hadn't clapped
his slender, pre-teen hands,
It's time to go give Grandma some love
he proclaimed, making me
but a particle adrift
in the dome of his greater compassion,
the vast and selfless amplitude
of a boy's better heart.
So here we are,
dazzled by Vanna White's smile,
her scarlet sequined gown
and seething cleavage,
our eyes lighting up
as the contestants lean
to twirl the neon dial
like ravenous leopards
from the shadowed brush
of mortal desire. One theory holds

that physical touch
promotes longer life,
lowers blood pressure, opens chakras,
keeps endorphins flowing,
boosting the immune system
which may or may not be the equivalent
of Rilke's call to
throw armfuls of emptiness
out to the spaces, maybe the birds will sense
the expanded air, flying more freely—
birds, perhaps, being blood
and blood being life? So when
the orderly scuffles into the room
with spare wheelchairs to sit in,
we cozy up to Grandma and Pat Sajak,
mindful to touch her arms,
her gnarled hands, to gently
stroke her twiggy wrists,
especially the left one
with a grape-juice-stain-colored bruise
from her recent IV ordeal
and in this way, possibly coax her
past the 95 year-old end zone line
to a centenarian touch down. So what
if her brain
is a sketchy silhouette
of its former incarnation,
the synaptical arrow landing most go rounds
on the black bankrupt
and lose-a-turn slots.

She can't remember
the old stories she loved to tell,
the wild, depression-era days
on a Nebraska farm,
the lousy ex-husband
who got hacked like pickled hog,
slipping under the chugging train
he was trying to jump, stone drunk.
Gone, gone, the impromptu kitchen
lessons: Chicken Paprikash,
recipes for stuffed cabbage
and pistachio cake, Mile High Pie
made with soda crackers and Dream Whip,
the hundreds of doughy spätzle
I've watched her shove off the cliff
of a gleaming spoon
like crazed lemmings
into a salty boiling pot,
watched them sink
to the bottom and bob back up,
the steam pinking my cheeks
as I sucked my lip in anticipation
of dumpling clouds
soaked in butter, paprika, cream,
the bright coins of carrots,
just the thought of something that delicious
spinning around your mouth
enough to make you feel
lucky to be alive.

IF YOU CAN'T BE WITH THE ONE YOU LOVE, HONEY

I think of Grandpa at the hospital,
talking for hours
to Grandma's long lump,
her wrapped body
turned away, slumbering.

After seven married decades,
the ardent, urgent fire
of his words, forging
eternal love. Imagine

the fervent notes
spilled down the keyboard
of her blanketed body,
this titanic speech,
a spontaneous eruption
from his reserved and quiet self.

Only to realize two hours into it,
when he rose and bent to kiss her,

love

that he'd wandered
into the wrong room

the one

and had no idea
who the woman was

you're with

he was talking to,

Honey.

In the Gardens of Esalen

(Ode to a Husband)

From the shady Eden
of a celadon umbrella
I can vow to emulate
the behavior of water.
I can watch the giant sprinklers
backbend for poppies,
genuflect for roses
like a woman in silver lame
doing yoga in the sun. Because
there is no wisdom like beauty
and here it is dirt cheap,
I'll take a seat in the dust
near a carved stone Buddha
holding court for a brood
of young succulents,
and I'll kiss your toes
in my mind
for staying home with the kids,
for slapping peanut butter onto bread,
the soft slices touched together
like palms in prayer.
No one knows
how hard it can be
and I'm sorry for the times
grinding coffee in the kitchen
you slipped a hand
up my shirt and I flinched.

As if your fingers, stray dogs,
had wandered onto something
private, sacred ground,
verboten land. Darling,
the stem of my love
grows tougher with time
even as the wind plays havoc
with my delicate parts.
I'll pluck myself
and cast me down,
a gauntlet
to the worms,
the musky hall
and teeming pipe,
the fecund depths
of your soiled post,
any day,
and like marriage itself,
let it feed, let it feed.

FAULKNER FARMS

We've come to escape the city,
the clash and burn of bills
and marital plagues. We've come
to smell roasted corn, apple fries,
a tinge of manure threading
the warm October breeze.
To taste cured meats
and berry jam, wander
a maze of dying sunflowers,
their wrecked masks
pecked blank by goldfinches.
Our children scale a pyramid
of yellow bales, rumps
sparking hay flurries
as they shimmy back to earth.
Red barn, black loam, the rows
of copper field pumpkins
like massive dented pots.
Huge, misshapen fruit,
they remind me of retarded people,
the mini herds I see
holding hands at the museum,
the big, incessant grins
and galootish asymmetry
of squinty eyes and slack jaws,
how I want to wrap my arms around it,
this love incapable of judgment.
I want it drooling down my neck.

I want it to arrest my heart,
strike me dumb like an incurable disease.
We are refugees, family of four
on the lam from everything.
A giant trebuchet fires pumpkins
at a miniature castle
two hundred feet away
and we watch as they splatter
into seedy oblivion.
I want it to suffice.
This day, the rust
and ripeness of it,
dust and grass,
my husband on his knees
spooning orange pie
into my mouth,
searching my face
for the look that says,
so good, it's so good,
beautiful fool,
give me some more,
I still haven't had enough.

NO MATTER

How hard I try to shake you off,

you who hold everything
in the glitzy tunnel,

where each line I clutch—
glass-grinding, threadbare, grappling
with shadow,

each jewel-encrusted temple, station
of the cross,
for us homeless
hefts
heightened meaning.

But you have a house

can sleep there, close
eyes and come to
the surface of orange. Only

There were some items I needed to see first

and got all optical again,
singing you
the demon butterflies,
their suicide teeth
wrapped in diagonal attics—
dusty string, Roman
candles that surrounded,

sputtering. Stacked attics
like Russian nesting dolls,
one inside the other
one inside the other.
But I have a house, I said,

many rooms, many attics
I hang ten along
the well-lit exit,
the silver shaped
like spidery diadems,
eyes in the rafters, diaphanous beams.
I kept telling you because

I want to make sure this really happened...

A bright ring
forged,
the void, threatening.

I have everything I need, I said,

this yellow arsenal,
the squash blossoms, each
tender fuselage
intended for stuffing:
goat cheese, basil, rough
flecks
of nuts.

No storm can touch
this love, my sea
of close-knit cells,

not even I
green, always green,
a green ring I keep expanding,

grinding the hours,
the milkweed garden
I replaced emptiness with
my smashed ring—
gone glass, planted
to attract endangered
butterflies
and all else pulsing
I tried to blind away,
only now I see you

and you,

you are made of everything.

ACKNOWLEDGMENTS

Grateful Acknowledgement is made to the following journals in which some of these poems first appeared:

The American Poetry Review, *Anti—*, *Atticus Review*, *Chaparral*, *The Cortland Review*, *diode*, *L.A. Weekly*, *Linebreak*, *Mudfish*, *Poemeleon*, *Poetry Bay*, *Poetry Flash*, *Prairie Schooner*, *Rattle*, *Red Wheelbarrow*, *River Styx*, *Silk Road*, *Silkworm*, *Speechless*, *Spillway*, *2RiverView*, *The Smoking Poet*, and *Valparaiso Poetry Review*.

"Black Guitar" was reprinted on *Verse Daily*.

"Faulkner Farms" and "My Bukowski Life" were reprinted in the 2011 Marin Poetry Center Anthology.

"Permeable, Smitten" won the 2011 Beyond Baroque Poetry Award.

"Persimmon" was nominated for Best of the Net.

* * * * *

I would like to express my deep gratitude to all my friends and family without whom I would not have accomplished this work.

To Philip: For your Superman arms of love and support. Thank you.

To my Beauties: Elijah and Vera Rose—boundless love.

To the Beloveds: Dorianne Laux, Joseph Millar, Marvin Bell, David St. John and Robert Olen Butler—endless admiration.

To Jason Katims: *Good pilgrim you do wrong your hand too much.*

To Kathleen and Bill and Brother John and Aunt Leslie!

Many thanks to Tim Kahl and the Sacramento Poetry Center for their original support of this work

To my Shrinks and Priests: Howard, David and Tom for
helping keep it together.

To my dear students and writing comrades especially Beth, Nancy, Ellen, Robert, Marcene and Katey—bless you!

And to Shelley Washburn and the Masters at Pacific University, Oregon. You simply rock.

—Amor Vincit Omnia—

www.ingramcontent.com/pod-product-compliance
Lightning Source LLC
Chambersburg PA
CBHW022116090426
42743CB00008B/875